Co
Colours

Written by Carol Read and Ana Soberón
Illustrated by Gloria Celma

Colin is a beautiful caterpillar.

Here's the rain.

Hello, Colin.
Look! My colours!

Hello, Colin.
Look! My colours!

Oh dear!
I'm sad!

Poor Colin!

Here's the sun!

Here's a rainbow!

Here are my colours!

Hurray!

Lucía

Activities

1 Colour Colin.

2 Find and circle Colin's friends.

Picture Dictionary

rain

sun

rainbow

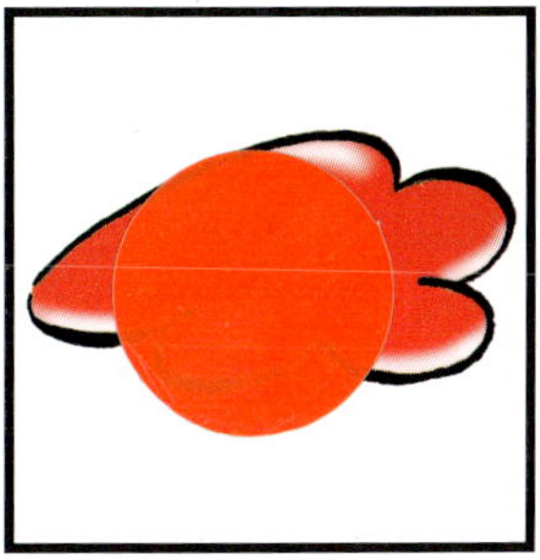

red

orange

yellow

green

blue

purple

Macmillan Education
Between Towns Road, Oxford OX4 3PP
A division of Macmillan Publishers Limited
Companies and representatives throughout the world

ISBN-13: 978 1 4050 2500 3
ISBN-13: 978 1 4050 5717 2 (International Edition)

First published 2004

Illustrated by Gloria Celma

Printed and bound in China

2011 2010
10 Spain
2014 2013 2012 2011 2010
15 14 13 12 International